001

002

003

004

005

006

007

008

009

010

1

*When witches abound
And Ghosts are seen,
Your fate you will learn
On Hallowe'en.*

014

013

3

015

016

017

018

019

Best
Halloween
Wishes

020

021

HAPPY HALLOWE'EN

Hold your candle steady
And keep a sharp lookout
For back among the shadows
You'll see goblins peeping out.

022

5

024

023

O let Us cast Dull Care away
Again be Children for a Day
Witches Goblins have their sway
T'is Hallowe'en, lets Joke and Play.

Hallowe'en Greetings

Spooks and witches are busy to-night,
Anxious to put good children to fright;
Let's get together to ward off the charm,
Laugh and be merry, and forget all alarm.

026

025

7

027

028

029

030

031

032

033

034

035

036

HALLOWE'EN

037

038

040

A MERRY HALLOWE'EN

039

Hallowe'en

"If in the mirror your lover is seen
You'll surely be happy on Hallowe'en!"

HALLOWE'EN
GREETINGS

042

"Watch your step" for it's Halloween

041

11

043

044

045

046

047

Hallowe'en Greetings

048

049

050

051

053

052

14

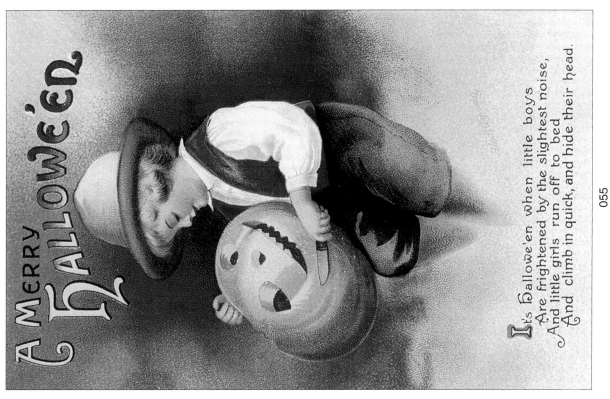

A MERRY Hallowe'en

It's Hallowe'en when little boys
Are frightened by the slightest noise,
And little girls run off to bed
And climb in quick, and hide their head.

055

Hallowe'en Greeting

Spooks and witches are busy to-night,
Anxious to put good children to fright;
Let's get together to ward off the charm.
Laugh and be merry, and forget all alarm.

054

15

drive dull care away from you
So the witches can't cast their charms,
Hang an owl's wishbone over the door
It will shield you from all the harm.

056

057

058

059

Have a Jolly Hallowe'en

060

061

062

063

064

065

066

068

067

18

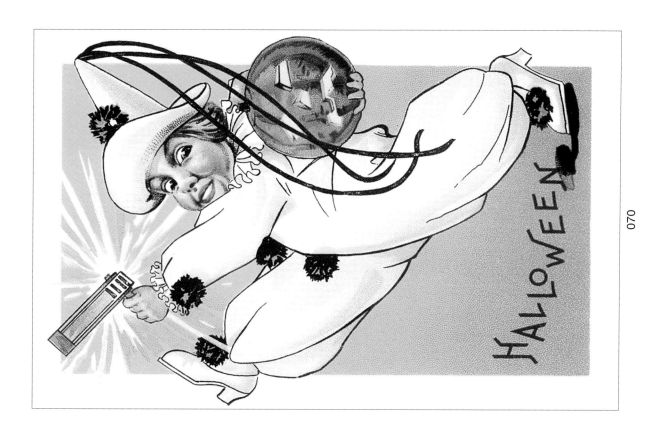

070

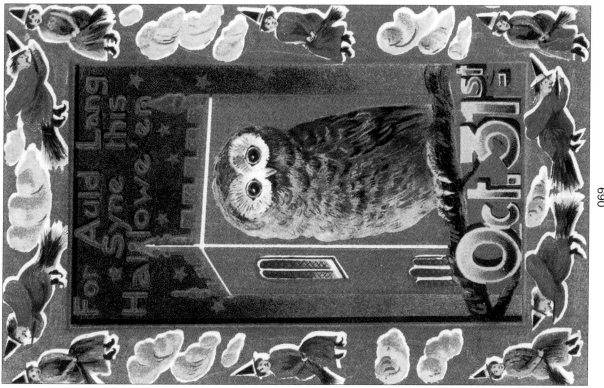

069

19

071

072

073

074

075

079

076

077

A Thrilling
Hallowe'en

078

080

21

082

081

22

084

083

With Best Wishes for Hallowe'en.

By pumpkins fat and witches lean · ·
By coal black cats with eyes of green,
By all the magic ever seen · · ·
I wish you luck this HALLOWE'EN

085

Hallowe'en.

086

087

088

089

090

091

092

093

094

095

096

A Happy Halloween
097

098

099

100

HALLOWE'EN PLEASURES

Of all the fun and
merry jest,
To "bob for apples"
is the best.

102

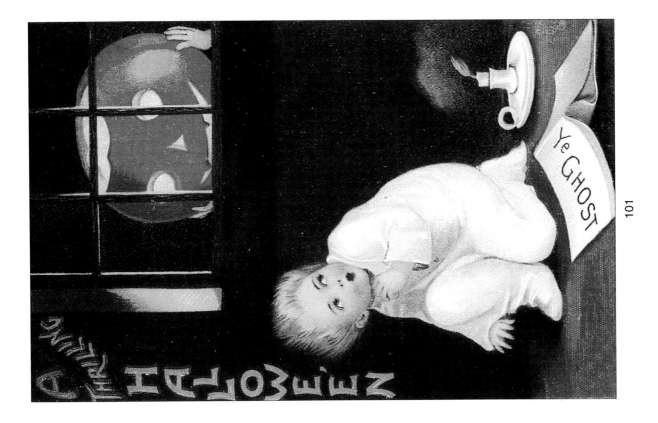

A THRILLING HALLOWE'EN

Ye GHOST

101

The goblins will catch you
if you don't watch out.

104

Hallowe'en Greetings

When Black cats prowl, and pumpkins gleam, May luck be yours on Hallowe'en.

103

27

105

106

107

108

109

Halloween
Greetings

110

111

A Hallowe'en merry, a Hallowe'en bright,
Though pumpkins make faces
and ghosts walk at night,
Let no noises scare you, and don't start to run,
For 'tis but a joke, and Hallowe'en fun.

112

113

"Cross your fingers
At the Witching Hour
Over Owls and Witches
You will have power."

115

114

117

116

All the signs of HALLOWE'EN
Seem to be about me.
I send this card CAWS I love you
Now really — can
you doubt me?

118

HAPPY HALLOWE'EN

119

32

120

121

122

123

124

THE HIGHEST EXPECTATIONS FOR HALLOWE'EN

125

33

127

126

129

128

35

When doubt and fear creep o'er you
And your heart is beating fast,
Look in a glass of water
If it's clear, the die is cast.

HALLOWE'EN

130

Hallowe'en Greetings.

131

A HAPPY HALLOWEEN

132

133

134

135

137

136

138

Be it Hearts, Spades, Damonds or Clubs
For o'er your Fate I'll ponder Well
And illustrate Hallowe'en Dubs.

140

WISHING YOU A HIGHLY ENTERTAINING

HALLOWE'EN

139

38

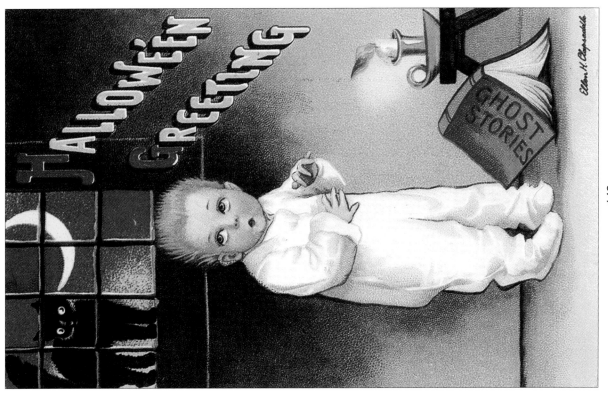

142

141

ON
HALLOWE'EN

Light all the
pumpkins·
and let their
weird gleam
Call Witches
and Goblins
to keep
Hallowe'en.

143

144

145

146

147

Hallowe'en

Pumpkin faces,
dance and gleam,
and Ghosts
walk by on
Hallow-
e'en.

149

148

150

152

151

154

153

43

155

156

158

157

159

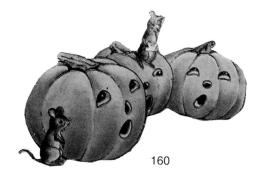

160

161

162

164

163

166

165

47

167

168

169

170

171

172

173

174

175

176

177

178